CON

MW00834758

Dedication

We dedicate this book to the Holy Spirit, who lives and breathes on the inside of each of us. We would not have been able to come together collectively to write this amazing book of testimonies, had it not been for the spirit of God motivating us every step of the way. Thank you, God, for allowing us to come together with such sweet harmony to tell our stories. Thank you for giving us the boldness to share our hearts with our sisters.

We also dedicate this book to each reader, each woman, each sister who purchases this book. This book is for you if you have ever been through a storm and you were not sure how you were going to get out. This book is for you if you are still experiencing a trial and are unsure of which way to go. We believe and feel that you will be strengthened as you read each page in Jesus name, Amen.

Introduction

We are all on a journey of some kind. We experience different seasons in our lives, but in every season, there is hope. He knows everything that you are experiencing at this moment. As you read this book, let God minister to you in every way. He wants to heal your heart, mind, body, and soul.

"I Am Created To Win" is a book compiled of 12 different stories, from 12 fascinating women who love God. Each chapter belongs to a different woman who shares her own specific journey with you. This is a book that shares God's redemptive power in our lives. We trust that each reader that picks this book will find themselves in one of the stories. It is our prayer that each reader is transformed and encouraged after reading this book. Our stories are different, but one thing remains the same, God's love and His promises for his children. We encourage you to see yourself in these stories. As you read this book, be strengthened and know that God is no respecter of persons. He has no favorites. If he did it for us, He will surely do it for you. We are all still on a journey. Let's be on this journey together.

Please know that we have already begun the process of praying for you. We may not know you by name, but God does, and it is our prayer that you are made whole today. It is our prayer that you will feel God's love and embrace as you read each page and each story. We boldly share our journey with you in hopes that you will be filled with strength and with hope. *Jeremiah 29:11*

Author

Letha Annette Young

Letha Young hails from Franklinton, North Carolina. She is a member of Living Word Family Church (LWFC). Her favorite scripture is II Chronicles 7:14

"If my people, which are called by my name, shall humble themselves, and pray, and seek my face, and turn from their wicked ways; then will I hear from heaven, and will forgive their sin, and will heal their land." (KJV)

Letha is humbled and honored to have been given this opportunity to share a chapter in the story of her life. May God be glorified in it!

Introduction

I Can Do This!

*Being **confident** of this very thing, that He which hath begun a good*

work in you will perform it until the day of Jesus Christ.

Philippians 1:6 (KJV)

***The birthing of a new home**: making the decision, creating the*

vision (conception), feeling the joy/fear/excitement, having morning

sickness (obstacles), hearing the first heartbeat, seeing the

sonogram, enduring the labor pains/contractions/birthing; and,

finally, the welcoming and celebration of new life

***Perseverance** - persistence, determination, grit*

Our greatest glory lies not in never falling,

but in rising every time we fall.

– Confucius

I Can Do This!

Those words are on a picture hanging in my office. Though the background portrays a darkened sky, there's a sunrise on the horizon ushering in the dawning of a new *unknown* day. It's simply *majestic*! Even though I inherited this picture when I arrived at my new office about 8 years ago, this year the words leaped off the canvas and grasped my very core as I completed purchasing my first home at the age of 55 (really, a week before my 56th birthday).

Let me start at the beginning and break it down this way:
The Situation, The Process, *and,* **The Takeaway.**

First, The Situation

"You need to get yourself a house. I don't understand why none of my children seem to want a home. You shouldn't want to rent ALL of your life! I always wanted to have a house of my own. You are paying a ridiculous amount for rent. You ought to want something of your own!" I can't tell you how many times my brothers and I have heard that monologue from our Mother. My Mother preached that

sermon for many years. I know that she meant well; it just *seemed* to come across as clear nagging. *To me, anyway!* I even remember telling my brothers one day, "I feel like just purchasing the house and handing her the key. Maybe that will make her happy, give her some peace, and stop her nagging!" *Why do parents do that? That's another chapter for another book (smile)! Now back to this chapter…*

After moving back to North Carolina some years ago, I reconnected with one of my childhood friends. She received her Real Estate license, and she began to sow the seeds of homeownership in me too. I wasn't really interested because I hadn't planned to stay in the area. I wasn't ready to think about purchasing a house. And, my *precious* friend came very close to nagging me as well.

I kept thinking, "What's the big deal about owning a house anyway? And, can I even afford a house? I surely don't want to be stressed out with debt. With an apartment, I can walk away in a year, but what about a house? Is this what I really want/need? Naw, not right now."

On the flipside, my neighbors and I began to notice that each year services were being cut, more restrictions were being added and the cost to live at our apartment complex continued to climb. I lived there for 11 years, basically due to the great location. Throughout the years, there had been management changes and challenges. Finally, the complex was sold. I watched this complex go from resort-like to slum-like. I no longer felt safe there. Finally, I made the decision that it was time to move. But, to where? And into what? *Possibly a house? Oh, that would make my Mom right! Hmm...*

In April 2017, I submitted my notice to vacate. My Mom had offered and convinced me to move in with her to save money. I thought about it. I prayed about it. And I cried about it. But I finally decided it was probably the best thing to do. So, I decluttered, moved my stuff into storage, and on May 31, 2017, I moved in with my Mother. That day felt like a heavy weight had been placed on me.

Now, The Process

In 2014, I prayed and sat down to write the vision for what I wanted and thought I needed in my first home. I made it REAL plain! I'd read, learned, and believed this scripture:

> **Habakkuk 2:2-3 (KJV): 2 And the Lord answered me, and said, Write the vision, and make it plain upon tables, that he may run that readeth it.**
>
> **3 For the vision is yet for an appointed time, but at the end it shall speak, and not lie: though it tarry, wait for it; because it will surely come, it will not tarry.**

I prayed over this vision daily, I began to declare this vision, and spoke it aloud. I began to thank God for my new home.

To appease my Mother, I'd done a little research on Home Buying classes. I didn't have to research for long. Flyers began popping up everywhere. _Free_ home buying workshops, seminars, and classes! Guess what? One of the first flyers came from my Mother (_smile_)! She'd gotten it from somewhere! And so, I attended workshops, seminars, and classes in Durham, Greensboro and Raleigh. My brothers attended some of them too. AND, I did begin to think that maybe one day, *when I'd settled down*, I might want a home. *It sounded good anyway, right!*

In March of 2016, I attended a Homebuyer Workshop in Raleigh. It was different from all the rest (or maybe by this time, my mindset was just changing)! This was an 8-hour workshop that featured various presenters representing the home buying process (realtor, loan officer, inspector, attorney, etc.).

While listening to the Loan Officer's presentation, IT HIT ME LIKE A TON OF BRICKS! I AM paying a mortgage! In fact, I've been paying a mortgage for ALL my adult life. But it was not MY mortgage! I'd been paying SOMEBODY ELSE'S mortgage*! (You know, that's exactly what you're doing when you choose to rent).* I could hear my Mother's voice saying, "I tried to tell you! If you had listened to me, you'd be in your own house. And, you'd probably have it paid off by now." ***Ugh!*** *(Smile)*
I tell you what, the realization and openness to knowledge indeed

equals power! It's funny, but when the light bulb finally comes on (or you recognize that it's on), it will move you to action! I was enlightened to the point that I quickly moved into action. I had to live somewhere, right? And, if I was going to pay for a mortgage, it was going to be mine!!!

Let me share what really helped me in this particular workshop: Instead of having the complete feast served to me all at once, I was served one course at a time (so I wasn't overwhelmed). I was able to digest, in bite-size pieces, the process by which to purchase a home. Most importantly, I learned that day that I would not have to '*go it*' alone. There would be a team of folks to help me along the way. *AND I exhaled!*

I hadn't saved money to purchase a house, but I learned that day that there were first-time home buyer programs out there to provide down payment assistance. That was appealing and a blessing to me! And, I wasn't about to miss or waste that opportunity. After the Loan Officer's presentation, I followed her into the hallway to introduce myself and let her know that I would be following up with her. She welcomed it.

So, that same day, I began to *envision the vision* of my home that I'd written about. It was a life-changing moment in my life. When I left that workshop, I left saying, "**I can do this!**" I felt empowered to move forward! That was Saturday, March 12, 2016.

I tried to connect with the loan officer the very next week. But I didn't get to speak with her until March 30th. I was very disappointed, but I was also highly determined! Perseverance!

The loan officer provided an estimated closing cost sheet to give me some idea of what was expected of me, and, what assistance I qualified for. My credit was pulled, and I was pre-approved. The housing industry was rebounding from the 2008 Recession, and I was told that it was a good time to buy because of lower interest rates and a good selection of homes. So, with my childhood friend (the realtor) and my Mom (of course), I looked for the home that I'd envisioned. I found the perfect subdivision. It was *close-enough* to

Mom and a decent distance from my employment.

I spoke with the builder on several occasions. He met my Mom and me. He and I reviewed plans. My home would be custom-built! I'd ride out to the subdivision at odd times, trying to get a feel for the neighborhood. I met a few of the neighbors. I even remember having breakfast and prayer time (in my car) in front of my potential home while on the way to worship services. *I named it, claimed it, and proclaimed it!!!* Yes, I had it bad!!! I just knew that my *forever home* would be in this subdivision!

And then one day, the builder started acting different toward me. He told me that he'd contact me in a couple of weeks, but a month went by, and I heard nothing from him. So, I called him. He said that he hadn't forgotten me. More weeks went by. I called him again. He recommended that I wait for the next building phase because I needed my home to be accessible. That cycle went on for months. Anyways, the light bulb came on *again*: this man did not want to build my house (for whatever reason). *By the way, the builder never did call. Maybe he was afraid that my Mother would move there with me (smile).*

Heartbroken, I decided to look elsewhere. I prayed about it (and no, I didn't ask God to **'knock off'** the builder - *smile*). I regrouped. After ALL that, I wanted a fresh start and a new team of players. I chose a new home buying workshop, a new loan officer, and a new builder.

In July 2018, I decided to purchase a townhome. I wrestled with that decision (*another chapter for another book*). I signed a contract and scheduled a visit to the design center. A good friend with excellent taste joined me for this 4-hour process. Thank you, Ann Wilson!

This is Chapter 1 on my journey to homeownership. Chapters 2, 3, and 4 will be told one day. But I will sum up by saying: As of March 2019, I am the new homeowner of a new townhome!

Hallelujah! THANK YOU, JESUS!

Finally, The Takeaway

Here are the takeaways for you to keep close:

1. Seek God for the vision – "Where there is no vision, the people perish." *Proverbs 29:18 (KJV)*

2. Once you make the decision, be persistent and determined. Perseverance pays off.

3. No matter your faith level, remember to say 'Thank you, Jesus! Hallelujah!' all the way through.

4. You have a story, and, your story is meant to be told. Help somebody by sharing your story with others.

5. **Vision** provides the possibility. **Prayer** provides the capability. **Workshops/Classes** provides the knowledge. **Perseverance** provides the 'refuse to quit' attitude. And, **The Holy Spirit** provides the outcome.

Lastly, I had my first family gathering on Resurrection Sunday (Easter 2019). I had a total of 14 guests! And yes, *of course,* Mom was there smiling all the way! We had a blast!

That has made the journey worthwhile! **Yes, To God Be The Glory!!! AMEN!**

Special Thanks To: **MY MOM** (*Mrs. Lether Y. Young*); my brothers (*Douglas, Anthony & Andrew*); Michelle (my *childhood friend & realtor*); Irene (*my sister-in-love*); DJ & Racheal (*my example*); Ann; Minister Mary; Sister Paia; Sean; Walthea; Arlene; Nykeshia; Gwen; Pastor Connie; Pastors Micah & Melissa; Yvette Bethea (*Best Makeup Artist*); Shequita; Linda; Vanessa; Howard; Nicole & Ronnie; Melissa; Steve; Cora; JoAnn & Gordy; Yadira, Shar'ron; Damian; Scott; Kayla, LWFC's *In It To Win It* meetup; *the Mighty Prayer Warriors at LWFC*; & YOU!

Author

Deborah Pittman Marsh

Deborah is a Raleigh native. She is married to Jimmy Marsh and they will celebrate their 41st anniversary this year. She has one daughter Michelle and 3 grandchildren. Deborah attends Living Word Family Church in Wake Forest, NC. *Favorite Scripture: "For it is by grace you have been saved, through faith - and this is not from yourself, it is a gift from God." Eph 2:8 (NIV)*

Introduction

Who's Your Daddy?

This is a story about a child growing up in a divorced household back when parents didn't get divorced. It is a story of how God used a big horse to shape their lives while equipping them for their future — navigating them through the financial hardships all the while showing them how God comes through when all odds are against them. How He provides for His children just like He provides for all His creatures, both big & small. During all this time He is teaching you that He is your Daddy and that He is with you always.

Who's Your Daddy?

Growing up in the big town of Raleigh, NC, was so much fun back in the 1960s & 1970s. My parents came from small towns in Johnston County, and their dream was to move back home. Therefore, we moved to the town of Pine Level during the winter of 1971. My parents bought some land to build their dream house.

While growing up, we spent a lot of time out in the countryside of Wake County. My parents helped with farming and the tobacco harvest, which gave me the opportunity to ride horses. It was then that I found my big love for the really big animal. I loved my cats and dogs, too, but there was nothing like a horse! My dream for the big move was to get a real horse, one that I could show. So, my parents got their dream, but so did I.

Our new house was adjacent to Mr. Gordon Peedin's property and Mr. Peedin was a rider and horse trainer. I got my first show horse,

Ben, from Mr. Peedin and he taught me how to show a registered quarter horse. We started out showing on the local circuit and Mr. Peedin also held shows at his ranch. By the way, this is not a cheap sport, but it was so worth it to me in the long run. I kept my horse at Mr. Peedin's stables, and in return, I worked as the stable hand, I fed, cleaned and cared for all the horses that he housed. It was a great trade and a tough job for a twelve-year-old.

My parents decided they could no longer be married, and they separated on Christmas Eve 1972. Of course, there was baggage that went along with that, but it is not relevant to this story. It was during this extremely difficult time that I discovered God comes in all shapes and sizes. Shortly before this their separation, my parents purchased a Youth Champion Registered Quarter Horse named Buggs for me. Mr. Peedin had trained this horse and rider, but the rider had aged out of the youth program, so now it was my time to shine.

Buggs became my confidant and carried me through some pretty hard times. After the separation, my mom learned how to drive the truck and pull the horse trailer. She even sold our piano, so I could show one final year- 1973-1974. The age class I showed in was 13 and under, so I only had one and a half years left in that age bracket at the time of my parents' separation. Mr. Peedin continued to work with me, even though Buggs had moved to our barn, I continued as his stable hand.

During this time, I lived and breathed horses. In the summer of 1972 and 1973, I barned tobacco to earn money for showing my horse and buying school clothes. Mother was working but made very little, so I worked to help out as much as I could. During this time, I had friends doing fun summer stuff, but you would normally find me working in the field or at the barn. Staying busy served several purposes. I could not sit around and feel sorry for myself as a poor pitiful child of a divorced household in a town where NO ONE was divorced. I had to ride and care for my horse every day. I was up before daybreak and went to bed late after all the chores were completed.

Mom kept the house, and I kept the yard, horse, our barn, and Mr. Peedin's barn running. Was this hard, you bet it was, but I was not complaining. I was getting to do what was promised to me and that was showing in the American Quarter Horse Association. Somehow mom managed to send me to Greensboro for a week of training with my horse and fellow teammates. That was ultra-cool, as we stayed in a strip motel and played poker almost every night. Buggs seemed to enjoy herself that week as well. I think it got a little lonely for her being the only horse in our barn.

In my mind, if I succeeded at showing horses, then I would win my father's approval and praise. As the years had passed, I did not receive positive approval from him. I thought that if I was really good at showing horses, that I would receive that praise and approval. As it turns out, I was searching for praise and approval from the wrong father.

God places a piece of Heaven in our hearts so that we will have the desire to search and fill this God-size hole in our heart. Over the years, we were churchgoers, and it was during this time that I asked Jesus to come into my heart and was baptized. You can say I was a baby Christian during the period right after the separation, but I remember feeling His presence in all that I did.

My parents' divorce caused my family to be a mess for many years. Mom and I moved around a lot, and I started working to help with the household bills as soon as I got my license at sixteen. God was working all this time to prepare and train me for the life that was ahead. The big plan was college, followed by a career. God and free will had other plans.

My husband and I met Easter weekend of our senior year in high school and two months later we went to our parents because we wanted to get married after graduation. Both parents shut us down because they wanted us to go to college as planned. God had a different plan and we got married in August of 1978. The following April, we were blessed with a beautiful baby girl. Yes, if you did the math, we were pregnant when we married. Little sidebar, we both received our associate degree later in life, so God still fulfilled all of our plans.

We do not know what the future can or will bring. Some things we bring upon ourselves since we have free will; however, if you are studying and seeking guidance from your Heavenly Father, He will not only show up, but He will shine through you every time. My mother had been sick for most of my life, as she was diagnosed with lupus when I was two years old. We had faced numerous times when she did not expect to live through the attacks, but each time God had pulled her through.

It should not have been a surprise when she had a massive heart attack nine years into our marriage. The heart was badly damaged, and they had to put in a heart pump to help her live and prepare her for heart surgery the following morning. As you can guess, this was back in the early days of heart surgery, but they were able to replace the mitral valve and open the arteries. However, due to her lupus, they could not get her off from the ventilator after surgery and the doctors told me that she would not make it through the night.

Even though we had all been praying daily, it looked like God was going to take my mom to her Heavenly Home. That last night, my prayer was a little different. My mom had called me every day and, at times, I didn't really want to talk but still answered the phone. After all, she was my best girlfriend as well as my mom. So that night, I prayed that God would let me talk with her on the phone one more time. The next morning the phone rang. I was panicked expecting them to say she had passed. Instead, the voice on the other end of the phone was my mother's. Even the doctors had to admit it was a God-size miracle.

God gave us another 14 years, so my mother was able to see our daughter not just graduate from high school but also college. She was at her wedding as well in 2001. God had a plan that none of us could have known. If we had not gotten married at such a young age, my mother and daughter would not have been able to have the close relationship that they shared. Our daughter was blessed and shaped by not only her four grandparents but also her five great-grandparents.

Everything that has happened throughout my life was and is to prepare me for what is to come. If this is true, then what is needed to receive the wisdom to survive in this day and time? That answer is within you and you only have to awaken it to receive all you need. Over the years, my relationship has grown with my Father and I'm not speaking about my biological father.

As we grow in years, so should our faith. When I was a youth, my horse and animals were my strongholds that helped keep me grounded. They gave me unconditional love, as did my parents, but my animals did not let me down. Unfortunately, that is not always true for humans. I say that to say that God has never let me down. I have studied His Word and activated the inner spirit within me over my lifetime. What do you need to activate the inner God within you?

You need to have a relationship with our Heavenly Father. In order to do that, you need to accept Jesus as your personal savior and ask Him to come into your heart.

> *2 Corinthians 4:4 (NIV) "The god of this age has blinded the minds of unbelievers, so that they cannot see the light of the gospel that displays the glory of Christ, who is the image of God."*

As scripture shows, nonbelievers have been blinded to the light of Christ. That is why you must choose to believe in order to live with His unconditional love and receive the light of Christ. Just as children crawl before they walk, and walk before they run, that is how our relationship with God works as well.

> *2 Corinthians 3:18 (NIV) "And we, who with unveiled faces all reflect the Lord's glory, are being transformed into his likeness with ever-increasing glory, which comes from the Lord, who is the Spirit."*

Often people think they must be perfect to be a follower of Christ. That is far from the truth because we are like a potter's clay. God is the potter and molds us each and every day. I believe that we are all looking for love and approval; however, I have discovered that unconditional love and life-long approval can only come from our Heavenly Father who loves for you to call Him Daddy. So, tell me, Who's Your Daddy?

I want to leave you with this:

> *Hebrews 2:18 (NIV) "Because He Himself suffered when He was tempted, He is able to help those who are being tempted."*

Just know Jesus will meet you wherever you are and make you whole. May God shine His light upon you and bless you each day.

> *John 11:40 (NIV) "...Did I not tell you that if you believed, you would see the glory of God."*

> *Ephesians 2:8 (NIV) "For it is by grace you have been saved, through faith-and this not from yourselves, it is the gift of God."*

Author
Antoinette McCormick

Antoinette McCormick is a wife of over 22 years. She and her husband Michael McCormick have one daughter, Michaela McCormick who is active in the ministry and serves alongside her mom and dad. Antoinette and her family attend Living Word Family Church. She is involved in the women's and children's ministry. Antoinette has a heart for people and feels that her calling is to build and uplift God's people. Favorite Scripture is Jeremiah 29:11

Introduction

On The Waves of The Ocean

"On The Waves of The Ocean" is about a woman's fight to stand on the Word of God no matter what. We may have a season that seems and feels tumultuous as if we are rocking back and forth on the sea. Our boat may feel like it is giving out and will not stand the tide, but God. He said in his Word that he would never leave us or forsake us. This story is about trusting in God and learning to depend on him completely. Let's dive in.

On The Waves of The Ocean

As I am sitting here at my desk thinking about a title for my story, I immediately thought of the ocean and the waves that come during high tide. I know that surfers who are skilled in riding the waves, like to look for the biggest wave to come rolling through, so they can immediately go after it, position themselves with their board and begin to ride this challenging wave. The thrill is to see if one can ride the wave all the way through without experiencing a wipeout. What is a wipeout, you may ask? Merriam Webster's dictionary tells us that a wipeout is "a fall or a crash usually caused by losing control."

Losing control is something that most humans do not like to do. We, or I, like to have some sense of control. For instance, I like to know that when I wake up in the morning, I will have enough coffee left over to make a cup before rushing out of the door. If I find that someone else in my house has taken the last of the coffee, I am not a happy camper. I like to prepare my clothes for the next day, the

night before and know what I am going to wear once I wake up —
simple stuff like that. I am finding the older I become not knowing
my next step can be very uncomfortable.

Well, the last four months, I have been experiencing a high tide,
accompanied by some occasional clear skies. However, for the most
part, it has been rough seas all the way. It is a scary feeling, not
knowing what may lie ahead of a storm. It could be rocks, failure, or
even death. Yet, somehow, I have been at peace while riding these
waves.

November 11th, 2018, I was laid off from my job. My husband and I
were living from paycheck to paycheck when we both had jobs, and
now we were faced with one person in the family working. How in
the world were we going to make it? That was my thought the
minute I was so nicely informed that I was being let go. Receiving
one more paycheck helped us for the month of December, but we
could not see making it through January. My husband did what most
men who are planners do; he laid out a financial plan that would help

us out past Christmas. December had passed, and we made it through Christmas. Now it is the New Year, 2019. I assumed that I would be able to find work by the middle of January. I had the faith to take me that far. We were going to be ok. Surely something great was going to open up for me. You know that saying, "when one door closes, another door opens."

The last Sunday in December, my pastor was in the middle of his sermon when he stopped what he was saying and turned to me. He began prophesying, by saying that "2019 is going to be a challenging year for you, you have already received instructions from God, and you are following those instructions. People are watching and will see how you handle yourself with the different challenges and gain strength by seeing your faith. You will be able to speak to the mountains and they shall move out of the way. I say this, to say that at the end of 2019, you will say that it wasn't a big deal." I must remind myself of the prophecy. A member of our congregation was led to write down the prophecies and after the service, she gave them to me. I look at it every now and then when the waves seem to get too tumultuous. January had come and gone yet still, no job offer had been made. I was at my wit's end but thank God for the Holy Spirit that lives on the inside of me. He has truly been my comforter.

I had job interview after job interview, and still nothing. I began wrestling with the spirit of rejection of not feeling good enough. My resume looked good enough for an open door, but I apparently was not good enough to walk through the door. These were my thoughts and feelings. I had to pull out every promise scripture that God said belonged to me and say them every time I began to lose hope, or fear wanted to step in. It is amazing what we as people take for granted when we have it, for example, being able to go grocery shopping and preparing food for our loved ones. I told you all in the beginning that I like to have my steps already planned out. We found ourselves not knowing what we were going to eat the next day.

I am a minister and was simply embarrassed to be going through the financial difficulties we were facing. My husband and I would be at church enjoying service all the while wondering if we were going to be able to eat. I would wonder if God would put us on someone's heart to give us a love donation, so we could prepare food that day. Our daughter never went hungry. We would have food for her, but there were some rough and painful moments. I call those moments my high tide. Praying for people around me, preaching and teaching, yet experiencing a high tide and not feeling comfortable to share. I had to rely on the word of God and His promises for my life. For instance, one of my favorite scriptures is ***Jeremiah 29:11-knowing that God had a plan for my life.*** I found myself repeating that scripture several times throughout the day.

February came and went, and still no job, or offer was made. I had one company that I had been waiting on to make an offer since January 27th. Now I am just mad. Mad at my situation, and dare I say, I had my moments when I was upset with God. I was worshipping, praising, praying, and confessing God's word over our lives, and I did not see anything regarding a job. However, I was still trusting God. Somehow, we were making it. It didn't make sense on paper, but our money was being stretched supernaturally. I knew it was the power of God and confessing His word over our lives.

I am over a women's meetup called "In It To Win It." We meet twice a month and fellowship. I remember one Thursday night there was a new member that joined by the name of Robyn. I remember thinking about how sweet her spirit was. I taught about the five fish and two loaves of bread. I mention to the ladies how important it was to trust God with the little, and he would multiply it with much. It was time to dismiss everyone, but before we leave, we always have group prayer. I asked Robyn to pray for me and I Informed her that I needed a job. She began to pray, and God gave her a word for me. To sum it up quickly, God basically said to me through Robyn that He had greater than what I was looking for. She began to say that God had me in a transition season and that I was going to take on a new role. A role that I was not looking for. She informed me that it was going to be greater than I thought, and all I had to do was thank God until the blessing manifested itself to me. She also said that God was going to provide for me as well.

Well, some time went by, and it is now August, and I am still without a permanent job. I am going strong with my women's ministry and my preaching and teaching, but my life is a step of faith. I am still riding the high tide, but I am not riding it alone. God is with me, every step of the way. This journey has allowed me to trust God and rely on him completely. It has taken me from wanting to know each step before I take it, to allowing God to carry me when I am not able to see my own way. I know that God has my family and me. The same way that God has me; he has you. Maybe you see yourself in this story. You may be experiencing a high tide moment. I am here to tell you not to give up. It will be ok. You will be ok. God said in his word that *he will never leave you or forsake you.*
Hebrews 13:5

It is September 2019, and I have been presented with two business opportunities, which will allow me to be in full time ministry. I would never have imagined that, which brings me back to the prophecy. That God was going to present me with an opportunity that I was not looking for. I am so blessed. This new opportunity has blessed me in more ways than one.   I remember it was on a Friday. I got down on my knees before I started the day and I prayed to my heavenly father. I was getting ready to tell God everything that I needed and how I thought I should get it. All of a sudden, I felt this urge to pray in the Spirit. The Holy Spirit just wanted me to let God know what I needed, and that's it. At that very moment, I stopped telling God how I thought he should work my situation out and I just prayed in the spirit. I trusted God. A few hours later, God began to place ministerial visions, and ideas for business in my mind.

I leave this with you; God said in *Deuteronomy 31:6 that he will not leave you or forsake you.*   During the high tides in your life, is when that amazing scripture comes in that says in *Proverbs 3:5-6 "Trust in the Lord with all your heart and lean not on your own understanding; in all your ways submit to him, and he will make your paths straight."*

My family and I have been anchored and sustained by the lord. He has given me grace and liberty. There is an unbelievable feeling that takes place when one must trust God wholeheartedly. Trusting God, even when you do not see your own way out. Emphasis on "your own way out." There is a popular poem that I have been fascinated with ever since I was a child. My mom used to have it hanging up on the wall in her living room. The title was Footprints. This poem had an image of footprints on the sands of a beach. ***The author is having a conversation with his friend. He mentions that each time he seems to be experiencing the worst situations in life, he notices that there is only one set of footprints. The other man replied that is when I am carrying you.*** We know that other man to be Jesus.

I encourage you today to let Jesus carry you in your deepest season of need. As Jesus carries you, I need you to use your voice and continue to speak life, the scriptures of God over your life daily, until you see the manifestation in the natural. God wants to know you in a deeper way. He wants you to allow Him to take care of you while you are on the waves of the ocean.

Author

Carole Riffle

A Native of New York for over 40 years, now a Carolinian is living in North Carolina for 15 years. She has raised two children and now has 8 grandchildren, 6 boys and 2 girls. She attends Living Word Family Church, where she serves whole-heartedly on the women's ministry and outreach team.

Introduction

From Addiction to Redemption

From Addiction to Redemption is about a woman that was spiraling out of control with drug abuse, physical abuse, verbal abuse, and mental abuse. This story is about God's redeeming power. It lets us know that he can make something out of nothing. Please go with me and see what the redemptive blood of Jesus Christ did for a sinner like me.

From Addiction to Redemption

My story starts off at a very early age, and how I went from being a good kid to a life that involved drugs, prostitution, juvenile facilities, prison, and psychiatric wards. I started with marijuana. My friends and I were smoking pot every day. We went to school high and smoked every single day. I went to Catholic school and did well, even high. I really got out of hand because my parents both worked. I got so out of hand; my parents didn't know what to do with me.

Finally, I was caught and sent to a juvenile facility for almost a year. When I returned home after juvenile detention, I went to public school. I did well for a while but started riding with a motorcycle club, and I loved it. I wasn't afraid of anything or anybody. I continued to stay around drugs and weapons. It didn't faze me at all, and since my parents both worked, I did what I pleased. Before I knew it, I was completely out of control again.

As I mentioned earlier, I was not only around drugs but also weapons. I became a completely different person. I had no fear of anything or anyone. A few years passed and I found myself arrested again. This time I went to jail on possession and weapons charges. After spending months in jail, I was placed on probation for a year. I went back to school and got my GED. I did well for a while. I was able to get a good job. I did so well that I was able to get off probation without any conflicts.

Once again, drugs came back into my life, and things went downhill. I lost my good job and started using LSD. I would be up for days, going without sleep. It was so hard for me to relax enough to go to sleep, I had to pick a new drug, heroin, to bring me back down from my high so I could get some rest. I lost not only days, I also lost myself in the process of all the drugs. I truly lost my mind. I was taken to the psychiatric ward for several weeks. Once released, I became an outpatient for a while.

However, that is not the end of my drug addiction. It started over again. I just couldn't stay away from it. Once you take drugs, it is so hard to stop. It feels as if it is lurking and waiting for its next victim, and that the victim was usually me. I didn't want to stop, oh I tried, but apparently not hard enough. So now it wasn't just heroin. It was cocaine too. So, after years of drug abuse, I decided to go on methadone. I stayed on the program a few years but was still a complete mess. I did, however, meet my husband at the methadone clinic. For the first three years, everything seemed to be fine. We were off the program and I felt my life was about to change. Well, it did. We were happy and even got married. Our life was good. I got pregnant and was so excited. However, shortly after I got pregnant, I miscarried. Within three years, I had four miscarriages. By this time, I was devastated. Thinking I would never have a child of my own, I did drugs yet again to ease my pain. Tommy, my husband, followed my path of self-destruction by using as well.

We began to sell drugs on consignment to support our habits, and that was our life for a while. We were making money, but not enough, so we moved in with my parents. One night detectives came to the house and arrested us both. I will never forget the look on my mother's face, the tears, disappointment, and sadness. Our bail was $50,000 each and we could not make bail. We finally went to court after being locked up for two years. We plead no contest and time served and we were released that day. We stayed at my parent's house. Tommy got a job and I got pregnant. Finally, this pregnancy stuck, and I had a beautiful baby girl. Everything was good. However, Tommy started drinking and at first, it wasn't bad; but gradually, he got worse. Then, I got pregnant again. I was thrilled, but my husband's drinking got even worse and he became verbally and physically abusive.

I recall a time when Tommy and I were separated because his drinking was too bad for him to be around our daughter and he caught me outside visiting a friend. When Tommy saw me, he ran over to me and beat me so bad. I had two black eyes, a broken nose, and a concussion. I almost lost my son. He was arrested and he did time for that. After I had my son, I was a complete mess again. I went back to using heroin. The addiction was so strong that I did something I never thought I would ever do. What I am about to tell you is my deepest and darkest secret.

I became a prostitute. This is my darkest secret that I kept deep in my soul. There were four of us girls. We were called his wives-in-law, but we were still prostitutes. We belonged to one man and one man alone. I never thought I would ever go, but I did. We had nice clothes and all the drugs we needed but we paid a heavy price. We were beaten often, but that's the price you pay when you are hooked on drugs. My sister had my son and my brother took my daughter. I couldn't be a mother to them. This went on for over two years. Then, the man was arrested. I am not sure what else he did, but he got twenty-five years. So, we were finally free. Free from all the beatings we took over those two years. If we thought of leaving this man, he would have killed us. Now I was free from him, but not free from the drugs. So, now alone, I went back on the methadone program. After a few months of being on the program, I got another job, and I was finally doing well again. I was free from abuse and drugs.

After working for almost a year, I managed to save enough money for an apartment. My sister still had my son, but she got pregnant. It was a hard pregnancy, so she could no longer take care of my son, so I finally got him back. I had a long talk with my brother and got my daughter back also. Finally, life was good. I was off the program, had a job and my life was coming together.

Then, a little over a year later, my husband got parole and found us. I was completely shocked when he came knocking on my door. All he said was I want to see my kids. So, I let him in the house to visit them. We talked for hours. I made him dinner and it was nice. We were a family that night. I had to think long and hard about letting him back into our lives again. Well, he moved back in. We were a family again for a while; however, Tommy started drinking again. It only took a few months for the verbal and physical abuse to start back again. This time I just wanted a divorce. I had to move back with my mom. It got so bad that I needed to issue a court order for protection and a few days after that I received a phone call. Tommy slit his wrist. His body was found by a friend. I went to the house where he was, and blood was everywhere. My thought at the time, was what have I done? Tommy was not dead yet, but close to it. A week later, I received a call from the hospital that Tommy was dead. I was devastated. I blamed myself for his death. I just wanted to be numb and not feel anything, so I started taking pills. After the funeral, I got some more pills, and this new habit went on for months. My kids were always with my mom.

I can't tell you how many times I overdosed. The doctors at the ER knew me very well because I overdosed that many times; but I continued to take pills. It was endless. Then, somehow, I got pregnant. I just couldn't have this baby. I did the unthinkable. I had an abortion. After wanting a child for so many years, I murdered one; which only made me worse. I had one more overdose at Central Park. I was found in the park raped and left for dead. My body temperature was 76 degrees when the park police found me.

I was placed on a respirator for life support. I was in a coma for three days. The doctors told my mother that I might have some brain damage. However, God had other plans for me. After three days, I opened my eyes, and at the foot of my bed, I saw a man. I tried to focus, so I turned away, but there he was again. It was Jesus Christ. I remember the doctors came running in the room. I remember seeing the disbelief on their faces. Here I was, in a coma for three days, and now I am being taken off the respirator. Two days later, I walked out of the hospital to my brother's house. There, my sister in law brought me in to see her pastor. After a long talk, I received Jesus into my heart and never took another drug. Over thirty years now, and I am a spirit-filled Christian who thanks God every day for being with me.

He has given this sinner a second chance of life. I am so grateful that I serve a God who took me from drug addiction, prostitution, and having an abortion -- to a life where I only want to serve Him completely for the rest of my life. He truly is a God of second chances. His mercy endures forever. I was able to raise my children in the church. I am a person of worth. I have forgiven myself for everyone I have hurt. My friends, family, and even the child I murdered. So much pain I caused myself and so many others, but especially my husband. I was never able to remarry. My life is filled with love for God and love for those out there who are still hurting. I thank the Father each day that I am now complete. I am complete because God is with me every day and I stand on His word, His promises, and His unconditional love.

If you have a loved one who has these issues, forgive them, love them, pray for them, and never give up on them. This story is a story of hope and the love of God. He never gave up on me; God is a God of mercy, compassion, and love. I pray my story will inspire you and give you hope.

Well, I put it all out there. I lost years of my life, but God has given me back so much more. I implore you never to give up hope. God is always listening.

Author

Gwen Moore

I was born, raised, and educated in Bridgeport, Connecticut. I moved to Raleigh, North Carolina, in November 2004. I currently reside in Indian Land South Carolina. I have been a Registered Nurse for 32 years, having worked in a variety of settings. I am the proud mother of Sean and Adria and the Momma-honey of Jadin, Gabrielle, RJ, Kai, and Andrew.

Introduction

SHY

This is a story of how a shy girl overcame with the help of God's love.

SHY

I was afraid to step out always thinking I would mess things up. I was keeping everything in -- the good, the bad, and ugly. Never feeling I measured up but continuing to seek my parent's approval and volunteering for everything, whether I could do it or not. Well, how would I know if I did not at least try? Approval. I needed approval but did not know where it would come; what I did know was that I wanted to be more confident and comfortable in my own skin. My shyness caused me to go into a shell. My shell was a place of solitude where there was no right or wrong, no one to criticize me or look at me indifferently.

My parents moved from South Carolina to Connecticut and worked very hard to provide for us. Our house was the place everyone congregated for big Sunday dinners. Family that visited from other states always stayed at our house. At times, our house was noisy and crowded, and I had nowhere to go except into my shell. The more family that was present, the deeper I would go into my shell.

No one knew my innermost thoughts except me. I only showed the family what I wanted them to see. It was comfortable for me. I felt safe, not sharing my thoughts. I did well in school and tried out for different groups and organizations; no one ever noticed how shy I really was. My classmates thought I had it all together because that is what I showed them. As I began to date in high school, the most handsome and popular guy who everyone wanted to date asked me out for a date. Really! Me on a date with the most popular person in high school? Shy Gwen, no way, what did he see in me? I would see him in the hallway, surrounded by a crowd, and I would keep walking to class. Was this some diabolical plot or a joke? It was so unbelievable, all of this emotion and uncertainty in the midst of my shyness. I felt something different that I had never felt before it was weird. My shyness was being invaded, and it did not feel good.

I was always involved heavily in the church; it was not optional. This meant I was expected to be involved in Sunday school, junior usher board, youth choir, junior missionaries, Christian youth fellowship, conferences, and conventions. There was never a dull moment; I was expected to show up and be active. Although I was active, I just went through the motions and acted as I was expected to. I met a lot of young people from other churches that I became friendly with and this worked for me because I did not see them often, so I didn't feel out of my element and they really didn't know me.

My shyness caused me pain and undue suffering because I would not share what I was going through with anyone, even my parents. As far as they knew I had it all together, or did I? Hiding and silence never work. I found that out the hard way. My shyness caused me always to question everything I ever did. Was it good enough? Did I miss anything? What ifs? What will others say? I felt better staying in the background, keeping a low profile, and not stirring the pot. After all, if it was a flop don't look at me. I am the shy one.

When I became saved and accepted the Lord as my Savior, that is when everything changed in my life, I felt a newness like I had never felt before. I stated earlier about the diabolical plot or joke; I knew this was not a joke. My spirit man was immediately energized, and I felt lighter like a burden had been lifted. I felt free! You don't know what you don't know. I knew there was something different about me, but I didn't know what to do or how to handle what I was feeling. God's grace and mercy helped me through the process of this newfound joy I was experiencing. I was hesitant to tell others of my joy because I did not want others to know what I was experiencing. I wanted to keep it to myself, not to be selfish, but my shyness was not completely gone. I have come to realize once we are saved the things that trouble us are not gone overnight. It is a process of reading the Word, trusting God, being in fellowship with other believers, and working in His kingdom.

As I matured in the Word and the things of God, I could feel and sense a difference within me. I became more vocal, and I would engage in conversation with others more readily. Slowly but surely there was a lifting of my head, and spirit. God gave me the words to speak; there were times I surprised myself in what I was saying. He also gave me a boldness and confidence to speak his Word to those who needed words of encouragement, words of life.

Being a nurse has been one of the greatest things God has done in my life. The shyness I once struggled with became no more. As a nurse, you are communicating all the time with patients, families, and co-workers. I found the more I talked, the more at ease and confident I became. Sharing with my patients and families became routine, and God would always give me the exact words that needed to be said.

Shyness is no longer a part of my DNA. It is said, when we know better, we should do better. My shyness taught me what things were not of God. He wants us to share with other believers and not keep things in. God wants us to be part of His family and spread His good news. God wants us to be bold, steadfast, and immovable. As I share my moments of thoughts with you, I pray you have been encouraged. I pray something I have shared will move you to your next level in what God has for you. Don't hold back, let go, the best is yet to come.

Blessings

Author

Melanie Caronna

It was not "MY" responsibility to "FIX" my husband, but to just love him for better or worse. My responsibility was to fix myself, grow stronger in the Lord, lay the rest at the foot of the cross, and basically "Let Go, Let God"! This became my motto. I was instantly "At Peace" with my marriage and no longer bitter and angry.

Introduction

Even Though Everything

Even Though Everything is a story about a selfless and undying love between a wife and her husband. Even Though Everything is a story of a woman that never gave up on God or her husband, it is a story of perseverance and faith. This story will teach and help you to stand on the Word of God, no matter what it may look like.

Even Though Everything

Even though everything......this is something my husband has said to me so many times over the past 17+ years. In September of 2019, we will have been married 18 years. I would love to say that it has been a glorious 18 years BUT...through this chapter you will see how that just simply has not been the case. But God!!

Just a little back story.... Josh and I both worked at the mail house that I currently still work at. I worked up front in the office, and he was a machine operator out on the work floor. When he met me, he told all of "his girls" that worked the line for him that he was going to marry me one day. The girls were like, "yeah Josh, ...sure you are. You know she's like 30, right??" He was 21. I had no idea about this. However, I did think he was very cute, so I would make excuses to walk out on the work floor asking questions about a work order or to post a check just so I could see him (especially if I were dressed super cute that day). A few years pass, and we are now 32 and 23, and I finally went to a party of his, and we have been together ever since. We started dating in March of 2001 and were married September 1, 2001.

We were so happy together. The day we got married, I was so overwhelmed with emotion that I could not stop crying. My brother and my Dad were like it is okay and Josh, poor Josh, is thinking, "does she think she's making a mistake?" and "why is she crying so hard?" But the real reason was, and I told him this later, that as soon as my brother took my arm to walk me down the aisle, all I could think about was that this man is marrying not only me, but he is taking on my 8-year-old daughter as well. I was just so overwhelmed at that moment, like who does that??

When I was growing up, I knew that I wanted to be a mom and have 2 children, a boy, and a girl. My 1st pregnancy resulted in a miscarriage, which I just know was that boy I wanted. My 2nd the Lord blessed me with a beautiful little girl whom I named Kayla. When I married Josh, he had a 3-year-old son named Donovan. I finally got the son I always wanted. Donovan lived with his mother, but he would come to stay with us some weekends. I was so happy, and I thought my life was finally complete with my wonderful husband and my 2 children, just like I had always dreamed.

In November of 2001, a really nasty storm came through which left the roads not safe to drive, but Josh insisted on driving to help a friend who needed him. I had a bad feeling about him leaving and begged him not to go. I just knew that if he left, something bad was going to happen. Less than an hour later, I get a call saying that Josh was in a bad car accident. The accident left him with a bad concussion and a lot of pain. For Josh, this accident started a downward spiral. The under-control substance abuse problem became an out of control substance abuse of both alcohol and pain medications. He has always struggled with anxiety, depression, and addiction, but I was so sure that because of my love and the love of my daughter and his son that we could save him from all that. The doctors had him on so many different medications that he simply could not function. It was like Josh was their guinea pig or something. They were constantly switching his meds and had him hooked on so many things; it was ridiculous. I lost my husband in a sense. Do you know that movie, *50 First Dates*, with Adam Sandler and Drew Barrymore? When I watched that movie for the first time, I was like "that's you, babe!!" In that movie, after she has a bad car accident and hits her head, she can only remember the past, only things that happened before the accident. She wakes up every day, thinking it's the day of the accident, and no new memories can be made. Josh was kind of like that, but not to that extent. He would just have moments of lost memory. He had random seizures in the past, but now the seizures were occurring more often. One day he confided in a Christian friend for support because he was hallucinating due to the medication he was on, and she told him that there were demons in the house. It was Christmas time, our Christmas tree was up, and at the time I collected ornaments that were ceramic masks. After hanging up with her, he was convinced that the masks were demons, so he destroyed my tree and all the masks. I walked into the door from work with my husband lying on the floor (I thought he was dead). Thank God he was not!

I never knew what I would be coming home to. Every day I would pray on the way home that he would be okay when I got there. My daily thought process was whether he would be okay, drunk, passed out on the floor or passed out in his car outside, and would he know who I was?? We went through a period of about 3 months after the accident, where he would have random spells of not knowing who I was. I would send Kayla to her room, tell her to lock the door and not come out till I told her to. I would then follow him into our room, forcing him to look at me. He is about a foot taller than me and at that time had about 40lbs on me, and I would hold his face and make him look at me while he was trying to push me away. He would be saying, go away please I don't want to hurt you, go away!! I would tell him -- you do know me; I am your wife, and you love me. This would go on for maybe 5-7 minutes, and then he would come back to himself and have no recollection of what just happened. When I think back on those times, I think wow how crazy I was, I mean he could have really hurt me, but I was scared that if I let him lock himself in the room, he would either hurt himself and or tear the room apart. I knew in my heart that he would not hurt me because if there is one thing I know, it's that that man loves me. He knew, deep down that he loved me, even if he didn't know me right at that moment or he would not have kept saying, "I don't want to hurt you."

Over the next few years, there will be lots of ups and downs. There were several calls from police stations, from hospitals and several trips to rehab places. None of them really worked. I would go on Mission trips and go to Women's Conferences every year and be terrified of what he would get himself into with me not home. Although, except for one incident with the police while I was at a Women's Conference, I have always come home to him being safe.

You may wonder how I got through all this without going crazy. Well, I thought I would a few times. So many people telling me what I should and should not do, it was making me insane. I spent so much time in praying asking God to "fix" him, praying for God to tell me what to do and whether I should I leave. I can honestly say, that through all of this, without the church and the Godly women in my life, I really don't think I would have stayed in the marriage. My friends, Elaine and Luan, were my angels at the time. I will be forever grateful for them for loving me and always being a listening, non-judging ear. People could say whatever they wanted to say, but they were not living in my shoes. I was so frustrated at everyone's input and for God not making him better, that I finally gave up and said okay God, I am done praying for him, and now he's yours!! YOU can fix him (you know because that's what God wants us to do right?? Tell him what to do?). At that moment, I was instantly free. I seriously felt immediately at peace. It was like God was saying, "Finally, Melanie, you should have given it to Me from the beginning!!" From that moment on, I just started praising God every morning for my husband. I would walk around making confessions over him like, "I thank you Lord God that he is healthy and whole," "I thank you that depression, anxiety, and addiction have no place in my home in Jesus name!" Every day instead of praying for God to fix my husband, I began to thank Him. I finally realized that it was never "my" job to fix Josh. My job was to lay it at the foot of the cross and for Melanie to fix Melanie and grow deeper in her love for Christ.

I was on a mission trip in Costa Rica one year and was leading the Devotions one night and as I was talking, suddenly, in trying to explain how much God loves us I said "how cool is it that God loves us…. Even though Everything". When I said this, I lost it!! When I said I lost it, I mean I was so overcome with emotion. It was at that very minute that I finally understood what my husband meant. He was always asking me, "Do you love me?" I would say, of course, I do, and he would always reply, "Even though everything?" It's funny how after all the hundreds of times he asked me this; it took me saying this in reference to God's love in order for me to fully understand why Josh asked me this so much. One thing I never doubted through all of this was that my husband loved me. Josh would then and, still to this day, would do anything to make me happy. He was just dealing with so much stuff on his own that having me yell and always be angry would just make his drinking and anxiety worse. Once I stopped trying to "fix" him. God completely changed my heart, which in turn changed his.

Fast forward to now. My wonderful, handsome, sweet, smart, and sexy hubby is a great husband and a great provider. He went back to school, got a degree at 40. He is an amazing OG (grandfather) to our granddaughter, Nailea, and an awesome father to our grown children. I am so glad I did not give up on him and our marriage. One thing I can honestly say is that I never stopped loving him. Even when I would be so angry that I wanted to crush a beer can or bottle against his skull (yes, I had those moments), I would still sit and just stare at him and think about how adorable he was. Marriage is for better or worse. And through the better or worse, which every marriage has, we just have to keep God at the center.

Author

Cindy Belavilas

Cindy is a New Jersey native, now living in North Carolina. Cindy was married for 24 years and is recently separated. She has three beautiful, bright, and talented children. Cindy is very active in several ministries at her church, Living Word Family Church. She is very deeply involved in missions, women's ministry, and the youth department. She loves people and believes in reaching as many souls as she can for the Kingdom of God.

Introduction

Walking Through the Fire

It's been a hard season in my life, and God has never left me, He has shown me Grace and taught me how to be a fighter and trust Him. I have learned to lean on one of my favorite scripture is "*When you pass through the waters, I will be with you; and when you pass through the rivers, they will not sweep over you. When you walk through the fire, you will not be burned; the flames will not set you ablaze.*" Isaiah 43:2

Walking Through the Fire

Everyone has seasons in their lives. This season in my life has been a really hard season, but God has never left me. He has shown me grace and taught me how to be a fighter and trust Him. Isaiah 43:2 says, "When you pass through the waters I will be with you, and when you pass through the rivers they will not sweep over you, when you walk through the fire you will not be burned, the flames will not set you ablaze." My story begins with my life getting turned upside down. I have been married 24 years, and it has been a good marriage, somewhere though, something changed. Life happened -- raising kids, paying bills, handling the daily chore loads and juggling work schedules. It pulled my spouse and I away from each other. We fell out of love.

This year has been hard, long, and full of endless arguing and not liking each other most days. Heartache has been a common theme too. Divorce truly is worse than losing someone to death. Only those of you reading, who have gone through it yourself, can relate to the kind of weight I am describing. It is the hardest loss I have ever felt. The only thing that makes that loss worse is when it seems as if they have moved on with someone else so effortlessly. Through this season of heartache, which I thought would never end, I will tell you of the pain of losing someone you have loved for over 30 years. Prior to the divorce, I felt a lot of emotional stress and depression; it was so bad at one point that I considered ending my life. I also felt a constant lack of self-worth, which made me feel unattractive; like I was no good to anyone. I felt it would be better if I was just gone.

In the midst of this season, I realized I was also dealing with hormonal imbalances. I took steps to fix these imbalances by realizing that I was wrong; it took many MD appointments and prescriptions. These imbalances impacted my sex drive, mood, attitude, and even my social skills and how I talked to other people. I felt very alone, misunderstood, and judged by so many. Even people I thought would never judge me, judged me. In the meanwhile, my marriage was failing. Although I felt alone in all the depression, anxiety, and suicidal thoughts; I knew in my heart these thoughts were not true. I knew all those things were lies straight from the pit of Hell. I came to recognize and understand my mistakes, along with all the stupid thoughts I had about myself and toward myself. I came to the realization that I did not "love me." It is a process to love yourself, a process I am still walking through with the help of the Holy Spirit who lives in me. He reminds me every single day, through His still small voice to just be held. I am never alone. I am good enough. I am beautiful and I am a child of God. I am His and He loves me, and He will never leave or forsake me. I have learned to be still in God`s presence and to let Him continue to heal what is broken in me. Trust me, I am a work in progress. God is still molding me into what He wants me to be. He is literally carrying me through this season of my life.

Through this season, I have grown and learned much. This season has taught me to be a fighter, to never give up and to lean on God in every circumstance. I have learned to lean on the Holy Spirit for He is my refuge and strength, and a comforter in my time of need. Satan has come to steal, kill, and destroy, but he will never win because the God that lives inside of me is bigger and brighter and will always be victorious. Although my marriage ended, I know God will restore all that was stolen from me. He also will provide my every need. He has always provided, and He won't stop now. My God is the God of the impossible.

If God can get me through the darkest and lowest points of my life, why would I choose not to trust Him at every other point in my life too? I encourage whoever is reading this, whatever fire you may be walking through, no matter how hopeless it seems, God is with you. Lean into His arms and relax in His presence. Let Him heal what is broken within you. He is a God of miracles and restoration. One year ago, I almost took my life, and He saved me. He saved me because He isn`t finished with me yet and He isn't finished with you either! God loves us, and He will never stop pursuing our hearts because He loves us with a reckless love. His love is endless, unfailing, never changing, and perfect.

Even now, although things are hard, I have peace because I know I have a Savior who loves me, forgives me and will never leave me. I urge you to find your peace in the truth of those same things. Trust Him. Trust me, I am in a way better place mentally, emotionally, and spiritually for doing so. I thank God every single day for continuing to heal me from the inside out. I am thankful for His love and thankful also for all the beautiful leaders, friends, family, and coworkers who have stood by me in prayer with such great love and support. I am also thankful, as well as, proud of my three beautiful children who have gone through all this with me and have clung to Jesus through it all. Without God, I would not be here to share this story with you. He is my rescuer and my guide. For that, I am most grateful! So, I urge you, if there is a story you need to share, and you are still here to tell it, trust that there is a reason. Maybe your story will encourage someone the same way I hope mine has encouraged you. Keep walking through your fire because what is waiting on the other side is worth the walk.

Author
Nicole Taborn

Nicole has been married to her best friend, Ronnie for 15 years. They have been blessed with two wonderful kids, Mikayla and Asher. Nicole enjoys spending time with her family, watching her kids play sports and serving at her local church. Her favorite scripture is, "Where you go, I will go, and where you stay, I will stay." Ruth 1:16

Introduction
Unstoppable Blessings

This is a story of overcoming Multiple Sclerosis, miscarriage, and fear while discovering how unstoppable God is when we let go and let God work in our lives.

Unstoppable Blessings

I just had my 31st birthday. I celebrated that birthday with my family, riding boats and wading in the water. I was never a good swimmer but just loved being in the water. We ate cheeseburgers, birthday cake and opened gifts. That was my 31st birthday celebration, and then life goes on as usual, right? Well, not quite. I went back to the busyness of life for a couple of weeks. I was going to work, going to church, cooking, cleaning, taking care of my four-year-old daughter, and being a wife. My health really never crossed my mind because I was in great health until the morning I woke up with numb legs. Both of my legs were numb from my knees down. I could walk, but I could not feel my legs when I touched them. I went to the doctor after a few days thinking; I lacked a vitamin or something simple. The doctor drew blood to check my Vitamin D level. It was borderline low but nothing to worry about. After checking my blood and not seeing anything pertinent, she recommended that I see a neurologist.

The next week, I saw a neurologist, and she recommended I do a spinal tap to see if I had Multiple Sclerosis. I set up the appointment for a Friday, and my mom drove me to have the spinal tap. By Sunday, I had to go to the emergency room because I had the infamous spinal tap migraine. I could not sit up without my head pounding. Once the headache was under control, I was able to go home. I waited on the spinal tap results, which were negative. Since the spinal tap came back negative, I then had an MRI. The MRI results came back showing several lesions on my brain and one on my spine. The lesion on the spine was the cause of my legs going numb. Soon after, I was referred to a new neurologist for a second opinion. My new neurologist reviewed my MRI and concluded that I had Multiple Sclerosis. I was shocked. I didn't know what to think. I didn't even know what Multiple Sclerosis was. How would it affect me? What would my life be like now? What does my future hold? I am only 31 years old. In absolute despair, I cried. Then I cried more until I couldn't cry any longer. I had decisions to make about medications and what would be best for me moving forward. With the guidance of my neurologist and support from my family and pastors, I decided to start a medication that would limit the relapses and symptoms of Multiple Sclerosis. Additionally, I was put on narcotics due to the excruciating leg pain that I endured from Multiple Sclerosis. I was still suffering and just wanted to limit symptoms and feel normal again.

During this time, my husband and I began to speak healing over my body and we listened to healing scriptures daily. Even on the days that I felt horrible, and symptoms were obvious, we continued to claim my healing over my body. After a year of medication and continued prayer, my medical situation became more stable. My husband and I decided we were ready to expand our family and have another baby.

Our daughter was five years old and if we were going to have another baby, now would be the time. I spoke with my neurologist who told me that I had to come off all the Multiple Sclerosis medications to help ensure a healthy pregnancy and a healthy baby. He told me I had one year to get pregnant, and if there was no pregnancy within that year, I would need to go back on medication to ensure my health didn't decline. I was happy to oblige. After all, it only took one month to conceive my daughter. Wouldn't an entire year be plenty of time to get pregnant?

Our plan didn't go as smooth as we expected. My husband and I tried for 12 months to conceive, but it didn't happen. I talked to my neurologist, who agreed to give me a couple more months to try since I was doing well. Finally, we got pregnant! We were so happy for that little at home test to come back positive. I confirmed my pregnancy with my primary doctor and was then referred to the OBGYN. We were so happy to be over that hurdle. My husband and I went to the OBGYN for a routine ultrasound. The sonographer saw the baby but could not find a heartbeat. In that moment, we were told that our baby had passed away. I was advised I would need a dilation and curettage to remove the remains of the baby. We were heartbroken. It had taken over one year to conceive our baby, and in that moment, the baby was just gone.

In time, we were over the shock of losing our baby, and we were ready to try again. This time, I got pregnant rather quickly. I went to my primary doctor to confirm my pregnancy. She confirmed I was pregnant but that my HCG levels were low. A lower HCG blood level can indicate a borderline pregnancy or problems with the health of the baby. I was told to return within a few days, to ensure the HCG levels were increasing and that the pregnancy was solid. On my return appointment, I was told the HCG levels dropped more. I had lost another baby. It was so hard knowing that there was a living baby inside of me, and then that life was gone within a second. I began to ask God why this was happening. God knew that I was on time restraints to have a baby, so why did he let this happen? In that moment, my focus was on the wrong thing. Instead of blaming God, I should have been speaking healing over my body and standing in faith for our baby. Looking back, I realize I allowed the enemy to enter my thoughts, making me question God. I had so much to learn.

After the loss of our second baby, I had a major relapse of Multiple Sclerosis. One day I began to suspect it was beginning to flare up because I noticed I was off balance some, but I was able to function.

The next day, I remember driving my daughter to camp. I was in a location that I knew very well then all of a sudden; I did not know where I was or where to go. I had to pull the car over and try to remember how to get to the camp and even how to get home. I began to cry, and I was scared. There I was sitting with my daughter in a parking lot, not remembering how to get anywhere. I called my husband crying because I did not know where to go. He asked me to describe where I was parked, and he explained where to go. I was still confused. By the grace of God, I was able to get home.

The relapse got so bad that when I walked, I looked drunk, I could not walk a straight line. I saw my neurologist, and he suggested a round of intravenous steroids to make the relapse end sooner. He also told me that it was time for me to get back on medication. This would mean trying to conceive would be over, and I would just focus on my health. I did five days of steroids as he suggested. My pastor called me to check on me, and he asked me if I was still listening to healing scriptures. I had to tell him the truth. "No, I haven't been." While my husband was still speaking healing over me, my focus was not on my healing, and all I could think about were the miscarriages. My pastor encouraged me to get back in the Word and to speak healing scriptures over myself. He was telling me to refocus on God and not my situation. I knew what I had to do, but I was scared now. This relapse was so bad that I couldn't work or help my husband take care of our daughter. I had to be healthy, right now, to take care of the daughter I already had. I was imagining a future of having to rely on others to take care of me, and I could not have this. The enemy was slowly sneaking in my mind and planting doubts in my faith. Fear began to manifest.

I was ready to get back on medication and just give up on getting pregnant. At that moment, I was fearful of what the enemy would do next.

Later that evening, I went to bed and prayed to God. He reminded me that His yoke is easy, and His burden is light (Matthew 11:30). His Word says I should give all of my worries and cares to Him because He cares about me (1 Peter 5:7). I made the decision to give Him all of me, all my worries and cares. The next day I woke up with a new outlook on my whole situation. I would remain diligent in the Word and was no longer afraid. The fear was gone that fast! I decided that I would no longer allow fear to stop my blessings. I would get pregnant again, and my health would be perfect. I would stand firm in my faith and would not waiver. Hebrews 11:1 says "Faith is the confidence of what we hope for and assurance of what we do not see." I had full confidence that I would have a healthy pregnancy. Within one month of giving it all to God, I was pregnant! This pregnancy was all I could ask for and more. My God said He would supply all my needs according to His glorious riches (Philippians 4:19) and He did! I had a healthy pregnancy with no signs of Multiple Sclerosis, and our baby was healthy. We named him Asher, which means happy and blessed. Asher weighed 8 pounds and 11 ounces and was 22 inches long. Praise God!

What are unstoppable blessings? Unstoppable blessings are God's blessings that we obtain even when the blessing seems far away and unattainable. It took me going through the diagnosis of Multiple Sclerosis and two miscarriages to understand what an unstoppable blessing is. God's blessings are unstoppable when we obey Him and allow His favor and protection in our lives. When I look back, I realize that the fear I experienced was so close to stopping my blessings. I had to decide to seek out God and give it all to Him. The Word says God gives us peace (Romans 15:33), and I am a true testament to the peace He gives when we truly seek Him. The Word also says that God does not give us a spirit of fear but of power, love, and a sound mind (2 Timothy 1:7). I surrendered to God and gave Him all of my worries, including the fear that the enemy put on me. God took my situation as His own and poured out His unstoppable blessings upon my family and me. I now have two beautiful children, a wonderful, supportive husband and walk in the perfect health that God has given me. I am excited to see the lives that Asher will touch. If I had chosen not to be obedient to God, Asher would not be here, and so many lives would be changed by that one decision.

When God has a blessing for you, there is nothing that can stop Him. Call upon God and let Him be unstoppable in your life!

Author

Georgia Goppert

Georgia Goppert is an entrepreneur/ multi-business owner in the weight loss and wellness industry. She served in the Army as a combat medic, attended college at Wake Tech, and spent spending 15 years as an LMT in 5 states. She found her home in Wake Forest and opened a Massage Spa in 2014 with her mom as her partner. She opened her first weight loss center in 2016 and her second in 2018. She has a passion for helping others. She was raised in Asheville, NC and resides in Wake Forest, NC. When she is not chauffeuring her two teenage girls, 14 and 16, she's attending women's prayer group and church at Living Word Family Church. She is currently working on growing her weight loss business (Infinite30) nationally.

Introduction

Hope Runs Deep as a Coma

God has delivered me through so much, but nothing compared to the time my mother got sick and ended up in a coma. With the direction of the church and faith, I was given a hope beyond the scope of medicine to witness nothing short of a miracle.

Hope Runs Deep as a Coma

There are many stories in my life that I could tell you. One was growing up in a government-built house which ignited in me a life-long desire to make as much money as I could to provide for my children because I never wanted my kids to grow up as I did. I did not know at the time that God would put people in my life to help me build my dreams, even through heartbreak. At the time, I didn't realize I went through pain for His purpose until I stepped back. It's very similar to standing in the midst of a forest and not being able to see the beauty until you step all the way back. Another story is one about my father, who wasn't there for me growing up, and this led me to want approval from men all my life. I was seeking validation as if I wasn't good enough. As the years passed, I witnessed God take over my father's heart and saw my father transformed into this amazing man who is in my life today and who dedicates his life to serving others. I mean, who would have ever thought looking back that someone could be completely transformed.

I could talk about what I encountered after I joined the military at the ripe age of 18 and how my experience was so horrendous, that after a year, I attempted suicide. Because of that moment in history, I can now see how God used that experience to give me an understanding of how to reach out to others who feel lost and hopeless. God filled a void for me through some difficult times. I could also talk about the time I lived in Vegas and got hooked on cocaine for 2 years, and even though I was completely lost, I still felt Gods presence. For instance, He got me to church one time, and as I sat there in His presence at church, He took away everything from my body I was feeling in the "coming down phase," and I felt wonderful while I was there. However, the second I walked out of that Holy place I got sick in the parking lot. Looking back, I realize now; He was telling me that with Him, I would and could be healed. He delivered me. I moved from Vegas and got to rebuild my life in ways I cannot even express. I went through a divorce and a housing crash that put me on food stamps. However, a car accident and a tax return gave me just enough money to help start a weight loss company that continues to change hundreds of lives every year. God was there every time I fell and thought it was the end, and He put people in my life that got me through it. But I couldn't see it until I stepped back and looked at the whole picture. Sometimes, when we are living in the moment, we feel like it's the end of the world not realizing it's all in God's hands - He is in control.

I want to share the one story that truly stands out for me, and that is the time when my mother got pneumonia and ended up in a coma. Back in late January 2014, my mother came down with pneumonia shortly after fighting off a prolonged cold. After a doctor visit at a local urgent care, she was placed on antibiotics, but they did not seem to work. I received a phone call from my mom a few days after she started the medication and noticed she couldn't catch her breath as she tried to speak, so I rushed to her house to find out she was in pretty bad shape. She demanded a shower before going to the hospital (that was work within itself since she was in no condition, but she's always been a fighter!). I barely got her to Wake Med hospital here in NC, and after assessing her oxygen and vitals, they promptly admitted her, and she seemed to decline each day. After three days in the hospital, she became septic. I never thought it was going to turn bad so fast that I couldn't remember the last thing I said to my mom. I mean in three days she ended up on full-blown life support! My whole world had turned upside down as she was everything to me. I mean everything! Now at this time, my brother and Aunt had made a short visit where I put them up at my mother's house.

As time went by, things didn't seem to get better. Her dialysis port kept getting clotted because she was unable to take blood thinners. Scar tissue in the lungs caused fluid to become trapped in pockets, so they had to do a not so common surgery called Vats with a specialized Surgeon. She was hooked up to everything. I got to know the good and friendly and the not so friendly nurses in the hospital. My kids came one day and we painted her toes yellow with pink polka dots. I tried to stay positive. I played music in her ears and laid on her chest to hear her heartbeat. Time went by, and at some point, the doctors informed me that my mom was in a coma beyond the medically induced coma. They did brain testing and scans and concluded that she had no signs of brain damage, but yet she couldn't function without a machine for every organ. Somewhere in the midst of all this is when things got heated between my brother and me. He didn't understand the pain I was experiencing. The dropping to the floor wailing, crying hysterically, and feeling completely hopeless. I felt a deep sadness to my core. My mom was my best friend, new business partner, super grandmother (second mother) to my two girls and well, frankly, she was everything to me. My brother didn't understand that we talked a million times throughout the day even after working endless hours side by side during the day in the spa. What he REALLY didn't understand is why I would post a picture to Facebook of me and her asking anyone and everyone for as many prayers as possible! I will never understand why he climbed through my mother's window and stuffed newspaper in the door jamb to where the door wouldn't lock. I suppose things happen when people think a family member is about to pass away. I won't go into too much detail of sibling disagreement, but it does play a significant role in this next segment.

So back to my mother. At this point, the doctors had taken her off the many, many bags of fluids and medicines that were hanging above her head. They finally came to me and said it was time to do a tracheotomy. I reluctantly signed permission. She remained on the machines after the tracheotomy, and all medications and fluids were stopped. I could see that doctors had lost all hope. At this point, they told me that there was nothing more they could do medically. Of course, I'm trying to figure out the best answer as I wasn't willing to give up hope. It was my understanding, after much time with Dr.Google, that once the "trach" is performed, then it's the end.

I wasn't convinced it was over for my mom so when Sunday came around, I went to church at Living Word. At the end of the service, they always offer prayer with the more established church goers known as the "elders." Now keep in mind, I have never asked for prayer from a couple of strangers, but I was pretty much game for anything! I didn't know them but wasn't shy about asking for prayer this time. I walked up to this couple whom I have never met and said I needed prayer for my mom in the hospital. So, they began to pray. The wife spoke in English, and her husband spoke in a foreign language to me that in any other given time I would have gone running for the hills, but this time I was willing to embrace anything because I was at my wit's end. (FYI- he spoke in tongues). After the "Amen" of the prayer and many tears, I opened my eyes and the wife looked right at me and said this is what you need to do. She looked and spoke to me as if someone gave her directions with no hesitation, she said, "you need to anoint your mom's body in oil and read 39 Stripes of Jesus over her body". I had no clue what she was talking about but was determined to follow any instruction or orders at this point. When I had clarification from her, I started to turn and walk away. All of a sudden she touched me on my shoulder, and I turned around. She looked me intently in the eyes and said: "And.... make amends with your brother." That put a feeling though my body, I don't believe I have ever experienced nor can I explain. What I mean is she didn't know me from Adam, and I didn't know her. At that point, I knew that had to have come from a higher power! I knew it was mission time as I felt I had a direct message from God.

Needless to say, I got my kids settled in bed and showed up at the hospital around midnight with my boyfriend at the time, and my good friend Katherine. We coated her body with every essential oil I could grab from our Spa. (The Spa my mom and I built together; remember I don't know what "anointed" oil is). We put it all over her body, placed a cross necklace in her right hand, and put a cross on her forehead with oil and the backside of her hands. (We really didn't know what we were doing, but it felt right). The scent was so potent; nurses came in the room telling us they could smell it over the whole ICU level and asked us to stop. By that time, we were done, and then I started reading from the book that lady from church told me to read. "By Jesus 39 Stripes We Were Healed". It is a little $2 orange book with nothing but healing scriptures. I went every day to read that book over her body and on the 3rd day, I walked in and did my normal checks. I asked my usual questions to the nurses about levels, vitals, any changes, and even pinched her toes looking for a response but of course, it was nothing as usual. So, I began to read. Then all of a sudden, I looked down, and her eyes popped open. It had to be the most exciting and freaky thing I have ever experienced. What a miracle!!! I started yelling for the nurses or whoever could hear me.

It's pretty much history after that, but it was very humbling to watch my mom learn how to eat, walk, and talk like a newborn. Today she is alive physically and spiritually. I am so grateful and give thanks to the church and all the people who prayed for my mama! Just remember, Jesus will never leave you or forsake you and WE can do all things in life through Christ who strengthens us.

PS - I ask that as you read this, you will pray for my brother and me to be reunited one day. Remember, prayer is power!

Author

Yulanda Henderson

Yulanda Henderson is a native of North Carolina. She has a Master of Arts in English with a concentration in African American Literature and Bachelor of Arts in Professional English both from North Carolina Agricultural Technical State University. Henderson taught English for three years between Guilford Technical Community College and North Carolina Agriculture and Technical State University. Henderson is currently working to release her first book and edits all types of writings for businesses and personal works. Henderson enjoys spending time with her daughter.

Introduction

The Best of Friends

Words are very powerful; and the bible says that life and death are in the power of the tongue. However, when we are talking among friends, family, or coworkers do we realize the fine line between gossip and attempting to help someone? What we say matters. In "The Best of Friends," Yulanda explores what talking behind people's back can to do healthy friendships.

Well you know she does not really like us.

What do you mean?

I think she thinks she is better than us because she is almost done with grad school and already talking about getting a PhD.

No, she is not like that at all

Yes, she is, and she is a church girl. She just hangs with us for all the wrong reasons. She probably judges us and thinks we are all going to hell.

I never thought of Yulanda that way until someone else said those things about her.

You know, she told me that Yulanda thinks she is too good for us and that she really does not like us. And I did not see it before, but I think she is right.

What do you mean, Yulanda has always had your back?

Yes, but she probably thinks we are helpless because she has degrees, a nice car, a wonderful job, she has her own apartment, she can pay all her bills, her credit is great, she has a good head on her shoulders.

Are you jealous of her?

No way, she is the one jealous of us, she is so two-faced and fake.

Yea, I think you are right.

No one thinks people notice when words are being talked behind their back. But, we do, we all do. When you care for people and friendships; you notice even the smallest change. Well, I will not speak for all people, but I do.

Voices change, they get lower, and disconnected. Eyes no longer connect. And I wonder, what happened to the person I thought I knew. The friend I thought I had.

I have always sensed when people changed towards other people, but it was not until I was grown and in college that I realized GOSSIP can change everything… even people's mind and how they choose to view you.

The old saying that words could not hurt was far from the truth. And I could not for the life of me figure out what I had done.

I rehearsed day and night different scenarios conversations, and nothing made sense; exactly what happened to make my friends change towards me.

It was not until I accepted a dinner invitation with one of my friends that I found out the core of why other friends had changed towards me. It all started with a simple question… do you think you are better than us? Are you our friend because you think you can change us? Are we projects to you?

I was dumbfounded. Where could such random and thoughtless questions come from and to be honest, I thought they were doing me a favor by being my friends. I was always the odd ball out.

I lived a very ordinary life, my upbringing was average, yet I was different. I was always different, and I had learned to be okay with all my differences. High school taught me that I was not supposed to be in anyone's "in crowd."

But it took the sound of gossip smacking me in the face where I realized being okay with my differences was just another way for me to mask my insecurities and hide behind my perfectionist complex. Nothing about me was okay and nothing about me would ever be the same.

What are all these questions even supposed to mean I asked with a very quizzical look on my face?

What do you mean what are they supposed to mean? They are direct questions and you are an English major; you are supposed to know what words and sentences mean.

Please do not come for my degrees that I worked hard on and if you had paid attention in any school you would know words are left up to interpretation, so please tell me what you mean by your words?

Oh, my slick mouth has always had a way of making people feel small; it was my defense mechanism.

You must feel like you are better than us no one cares that you make good grades all the time and you have a new car and your parents are still helping to pay your bills.

What, that is what makes you think that I am better than you now. So, this is about me getting into grad school, my dad buying me a

car for graduating and my name is not in the ceremony book under
any of the honor achievements. I still have not lined up a job because
what graduate student doesn't work and are your serious right now?

If you are not graduation with honors how did you get accepted into
grad school? And how do you know you are not graduating with
honors?

I don't know!

Well, why do you have such an attitude?

I don't, but I must go to a seminar, so I will talk to you later.

There was no seminar to go to; I had already finished my last final
paper. I thought it was at least worth a B. I could live with a B today
after that conversation I could have lived with a C if I was able to
stay in grad school. I could make one C; only one C was allowed in
grad school and I would risk blowing it on this grade and class
because my mind was racing about friendships.

Words, my goodness do they hurt. I would even argue that the
thoughts other people think of you can hurt if you let it.

I let people; people's words hurt me. I had a deep-rooted fear of
people and it started with the words they thought or said about me.

I needed to be accepted by people. In fact, why did I need a slick
mouth as a defense mechanism.

If the bible is true and God would fight all my battles, I did not need
to respond to every comment that was made to me or about me.

I was determined not to be a pushover though. People would not run over me, so where is the balance between being able to answer people in a godly manner and not letting people run over me. Or just be plain stupid.

God, help me to overcome or better just have people shut their mouth especially about me. I do not even talk about people. I listened that time in the 10th grade when I wanted to gossip to my grandma and she listened to everything I had to say, but nicely told me to keep other people's name out of my mouth because I did not know what I had to go through in life. From that day forward, I have not spoken anything bad about anyone. SO, why are you letting this happen to me. Why am I losing yet another set of friends? Good friends at that…at least they accepted me and did not try to pressure me into going out to clubs or to wear pants. Jesus, why do you take friends away from me all the time.

I should have been praying for another A or a new job; for goodness sake my apartment lease would be up in another month and I needed to find another place to stay.

However, words and stupid gossip consumed my mind and therefore made me pray.

I cried at the all too familiar feeling I felt when I knew my circle would change again. But now I needed to understand why and what were all these insecure feelings I never wanted to deal with. I could make new friends, but these feelings I really had to deal with.

I had some emotional wounds that now needed to heal and new friends to make.

I would have much rather learned this through someone else. I would have gladly been a friend to someone who had lost a friend, but to be the one who was encountering the trial was hard.

This led me to a different set of questions for God. Why do You have to use trials to stretch us?

Other people's words should not have this much affect on anyone. I did what I knew to do; pray. Just talk to God about everything I was feeling and read the bible. I was shocked when in my quiet time God asked me to forgive them and let them go. This friendship would never be the same and it had nothing to do with me. Or maybe it did. I was still unclear on what had happened in the first place.

Proverbs 16:28 became my reference verse as I talked to God about my big issue of friends. "A troublemaker plants seeds of strife; gossip separates the best of friends" (NLT).

Little did I know at the time of this immense gossip encounter, God was preparing me for a much bigger gossip lesson that would come later in life. I now had a point of reference to gauge when people changed towards me based on the words and feelings of other people. It also helped me to be okay with having to let friendships go.

The biggest thing I have learned about words is they have the power to change for better or for worse. And they come back around no matter if what you spoke was good or bad.

The biggest lesson I learned in life with this is God really does work all things together for our good.

God used these friends as a catalyst for other friendships that would break in my future.

Today, my college bestie and I are friends again.

In 2016, I wrote her a letter thanking her for allowing God to use her to teach me lessons about losing and gaining people.

My favorite verse in the bible is Romans 8:28, "…all things work together for good according to them that love God, to them who are called according to his purpose" (KJV).

God really does use everything; the good, bad, ugly, and gossip to mold us into the men and women He has called us to be.

Author

Reise Greenfield

A wife to Dave Greenfield and mother to Nathan (Marian) and Kathryn (Billy). Gigi to Lacey and Liam. Reise is a preschool teacher and active at Living Word Family Church. She believes, according to *Jeremiah 29:11, that God has an amazing plan for our lives.*

Introduction

The Provision

This is the story of how Father God carried us through three years of my husband's unemployment. He provided for our every need and blessed our hearts with joy, peace, and contentment.

The Provision

March 29, 2013 is a day forever etched in my memory. My husband called and said, "Guess what happened to me today"? I knew instantly that the company he worked for had closed and that he had been laid off from his job. Thus, our adventure began. I was scared and sad. Dave had survived all the other layoffs and company changes. How were we going to survive and pay our bills on just my part-time income? Dave was offered a job transfer to South Carolina. That meant we would move away from our children, my parents, and our new church. My parents were at a stage of their lives where they needed my assistance. I was concerned about how I could help them if I lived four hours away. We prayed and made the decision to turn down the job proposal in South Carolina. Instead, Dave would become a full-time student. Choosing school over a paying job seemed like an insane choice. But we had come to the place where we trusted God to provide for our every need. Praise God we were already tithers and operating under an open Heaven. This open Heaven would play a large part in the miracles and blessings that would occur over the upcoming days and years.

Miracle number one was the peace we felt about our decisions and the support we received from family. I had many opportunities to be afraid. Fear was something that I had to stand against frequently. Reading the Bible, listening to praise music, and good friends helped me to stay focused on the daily blessings that would fill the years ahead. Joshua 1:9 lays this out perfectly for us: "Have I not commanded you? Be strong and courageous. Do not be afraid; do not be discouraged; for the Lord, your God will be with you wherever you go." As we continued to seek God, we learned about several government programs that were in place to help families that were experiencing unemployment. As much as I didn't want to need assistance from the government, God used these programs to help us weather the storm.

Miracle number two was a tuition-free education at Wake Technical Community College. His new degree would take Dave in the right direction to have a new career in a field that would not be obsolete in just a few years. The program also paid for books and supplies as long as he maintained a certain grade point average and finished all of his classes during the allotted time. Dave had to change his days from working a typical 40-45-hour work week to being a student with classes and homework. He hadn't been a student for over 25 years, so this required him to give a lot of his attention to his schoolwork. The class and homework time cut deeply into our family life. I learned how much I depended on Dave to meet my need for companionship. I felt very lonely on those days when his priority had to remain on his schoolwork. It was not fair for me to place this additional burden on Dave. I had to grow up and allow God to fill this void in my life. God wanted to be my friend, but, he needed all of my heart for this to happen. Trusting him and spending time with him was how this friendship grew. While Dave's educational needs were met, there was still the question about how we would pay the mortgage and other bills. I worked part-time at a preschool and did not earn enough money to pay our bills.

Miracle number three was a two-fold miracle. We learned that Dave was eligible to receive unemployment benefits for the entire two years that he was in school. An additional blessing was the mortgage forgiveness program. This program was designed especially for families in our situation. It would make our mortgage payment every month over the two years while Dave attended school. Being assured that we would not lose our home to foreclosure was a huge relief! These blessings were huge. But God's love provided in many other ways. A friend recommended me for a babysitting job. I still babysit sweet children that I absolutely adore. During those two years, this babysitting job bought a lot of groceries and made sweet memories that will last a lifetime. A few months after Dave's layoff, my teaching job ended for the summer. The end of school meant that I was also going to be unemployed. God quickly opened doors for me to begin working for Home Instead Senior Care. It was an eye-opening job that allowed me to minister to folks on the opposite end of the age spectrum of my preschool students. It was hard and brought many different challenges. God used this to teach me compassion for a vulnerable segment of our population who are often neglected. Dave also found a part-time job driving patients to their doctor appointments. Combined with Dave's unemployment check, we were able to pay our bills. While we were able to pay our bills many of the extras like dinner out, new clothes, and movies had to be downsized or even eliminated from our budget. I realize that this is a "first world" problem. We had everything we needed, and a lot more than the majority of the world will ever have. But my heart needed a lesson in contentment. I knew God was providing, but it seemed so easy for me to slip into self-pity when I saw others enjoying things that I did not have. Wow, what an eye-opener to how shallow my life was. I felt so ashamed at not being grateful for all that I had. This led me to begin writing in a joy journal. It is so important for us to stay in a place of thankfulness to God and all He does for us every day. The journal was the place to turn when I felt sad and neglected. It kept me focused on the joys of daily life. One special blessing came in a rather odd fashion. Through a series of events, we became a one car family. Dave needed the car for school and work. A dear friend stepped up to the plate and drove me to/from the preschool every day. She would stop for me to buy groceries and always made me feel like it was her pleasure to chauffeur me around town. Finally, September 2015 arrived. Dave completed his classes and graduated with honors from Wake Tech. Yikes! A new faith adventure was about to begin. With our support ending, it was time for Dave to find a new, well-paying job. In

December he interviewed with a small company named Optricity. He felt like this job would be a good fit for his new skills. He began working there in January of 2016. While we still had financial needs, we were certain that God would continue to show us the path to follow. Recently, I was reading Deuteronomy 29:5 where it reads; Yet the LORD says, "During the forty years that I led you through the wilderness, your clothes did not wear out, nor did the sandals on your feet." Over the past few years, this verse has become real to me. God does love us and will be with us through every adventure. Trust in Him!

Author

Kelly Humes

Dedicated single mom, born in Alabama, but lived most of my life in North Carolina. I have a heart to serve the hurting and broken-hearted. I leaned heavily on Psalm 27:1-14(KJV) during some of my darkest days. It was my anchor.

Introduction

The Power of One's Words

Imagine a bud blossoming bold, a glowing flower struggling to thrive in the midst of an ugly, lifeless field of jagged stones, sharp thorns, and hidden quicksand.

That's my story of how the power of one's words can keep you in that dreadful environment or drive you to flourish, awakening authority and power over darkness, evil spirits, and even death.

The Power of One's Words

As I look back on my life, there are many things I would change. Knowing what I know now, my life would have been so different; however, I am who I am because of what I've been through. I'm thankful that God has kept me even when I didn't realize it.

Imagine a bud blossoming, a glowing flower struggling to thrive in an ugly, lifeless field of jagged stones, sharp thorns and hidden quicksand. Well, that's my story of how someone's words can either trap you in a dreadful space or drive you to flourish, awakening authority and power over darkness, evil spirits, and even death.

For as long as I can remember, I've never felt a part of my immediate family. Since I am the only girl with three brothers, outsiders would think I'd be cherished and protected; but that wasn't the case. I felt like I didn't belong. I recall asking if I were born into my family. That bond, specifically with my mother was never there. My father traveled for his job, leaving my mom as the primary caregiver. For all appearances from the outside, we were the "perfect" family. A two-parent household, both working, homeowners, two cars and well respected in the community. All I wanted and needed was love and acceptance. I felt my father did not protect me from my mother's destructive words. She constantly highlighted my imperfections. Frequently speaking harsh words over me. I was told many times, "you don't need to be eating that" or "you need to lose weight, you'd look so much better." Mom told me that had she had a choice she would have never had a daughter. Difficult to believe she actually spoke those words out loud. (Proverbs 18:4 KJV) That sealed my worst thoughts. At the time, my purpose was to do the chores and keep my younger sibling. As a result, rebellion and hatred spread within me like a wildfire. My 5th-grade year consisted of strict diets limiting me to boiled eggs, baked or boiled chicken and vegetables. No, I wasn't perfect. Didn't look a certain way, nor did I "act" the way I should have according to my mother's standards. Not feeling loved, lacking acceptance and detachment, my self-esteem evaporated. Suicide was a fleeting thought because I thought that I served no purpose. Thankfully, God never let that thought take root.

As a young teen, I would say, "I'm never having children." (Psalm 141:3 KJV) I spoke this over my life for years. Between my feelings of being left out, isolation and misunderstood, I couldn't take the chance of passing this to my child. I hovered between depression and anxiety. My comfort zone was behind closed doors, like my bedroom. However, after a while, closing my bedroom door was only allowed when I was changing clothes, so I moved my "zone" to the bathroom. My thought was that's a private place, no one will disturb me, but there was no solace there either.

My parents dropped me off at church and picked me up. I'd go with friends, their families or drive myself at age 16. I look back and don't understand why we didn't attend church as a family. Through it all, I didn't leave the church, the choir, nor the youth mentorship. I was a mess, I had no Godly role model or mentor in close proximity. But my aunt, who lived overseas approximately 40 years, is and has been a sister, friend, confidant and spiritual advisor. I've opened up to her more than she wanted at times, and she has never judged me. She has always been there with love, prayer and spiritual guidance.

My mother said to me earlier in my teen years that I would be the child to leave and never return. I left home at the age of 18, with my mind made up to never return. Although I would still visit, after just two days, I would be wound up and ready to leave again. Once I left home, I became very promiscuous. I wanted control of something in my life. I wasn't looking for love, so I thought. I married early for an "adventure" since he was in the military. That was my plan, not God's. The relationship was volatile. Abusive, both verbally and physically. It wasn't all him. I was extremely angry and bitter. I wanted a child but was told it would be difficult or impossible. My baggage from the past was draining the life out of me.

As a young divorcee, I overheard my parents talking about a young man dad would golf with. I later saw my dad speaking with a young man. It turned out to be the "golf" buddy. I rushed my mom

through checkout and made my way over to my father, but the man

had turned and walked away. I asked dad to introduce me to him.

He told me I needed to lose weight before he introduced me to the

young man. He didn't protect me from mom's frequent emotional

and verbal volleys; he joined her. I was completely devastated. I had

to separate myself from my family in order to survive. My visits

became less frequent. Once or twice a year. As I grew my

relationship with the Lord, I began to see and feel differently. It has

been a long bumpy road, and I'm still not where I want to be;

however, I'm not where I was. Praise God for not giving up on me

when I felt like giving up.

I so desperately wanted to be a mother. I began the adoption process

as a single parent. I became impatient with the lengthy process of

adoption and returned to a toxic relationship. I re-married my ex-

husband for his medical benefits, which covered infertility

treatments. I was a full-time student, one semester short of my

bachelor's degree. I was working full time and in an abusive marriage with a cocaine addict all while having weekly ultrasounds and hormone injections, trying to fulfill my plan for a child. On my last visit to the endocrinologist, I broke down crying hysterically, and after speaking with my doctor, I decided to stop treatment. I knew I needed to finish my degree because the odds were, I would not go back if I dropped out. I knew I needed to get divorced and leave the toxic environment. It was painful deciding to wait on motherhood knowing my chances were already slim to none. An old friend told me that I would not carry a child, but I would have a son. I was furious! I often questioned God why I was going through all this heartbreak. Alone one night, I cried out and heard his voice. I froze. He heard me! (Jeremiah 29: 12-13 KJV) He's with me.

In 2002, I was relocated by my employer. I thanked the Lord I was not laid off, but He sent me to a city I would not have chosen. His plan, not mine. Before my relocation, I had reached out to my caseworker to reactivate my adoption application. I received the call within a year of my relocating. I was overjoyed. Then she stated that there were a couple of medical issues and I needed to make a decision. I told her I'd deal with it, then asked, "When can I see my baby?" Three days later, I knew what unconditional love felt like. When I walked into the room and saw him, something came over me. I rushed to him and the bond was immediate. The brief visit was five hours. I couldn't wait until the next morning.

I got very little sleep for fear of oversleeping. My hour and a half drive seemed like a lifetime. Once there, I was informed that the pediatric cardiologist was available to meet with me. When I met him, my spirit was deeply disturbed. He spoke so negatively over my child's birth mother and death over my child. (Proverbs 18:21 KJV) He wanted to perform one more test. I refused. I requested a referral to a cardiologist in my area. I had declared life over my son.

Within days of taking him home, my child had a Dedication ceremony. He was born with cocaine in his system and no prenatal care. I was fighting for his life from the time I received my two-month-old blessing. I immediately set appointments for a local cardiologist and neurologist but had difficulty getting a pediatrician.

During our initial visit with the pediatric cardiologist, he informed me that the normal lifespan for my baby's condition was two years, but then added, "It's not up to us. God has the last word." I said, "Yes, we are in the right place!" I informed him we didn't have a pediatrician yet. He referred me to a friend, whose office earlier refused accepting new patients. I received a phone call from that pediatric office on my way home from the cardiologist appointment.

I had no problem praising and giving God the glory there in the office for Christopher's healing at 16 months old. His heart was normal size. He was released as a patient. His heart was not the only challenge we were facing. He had a seizure after birth due to traces of cocaine in his system. I had also met with a neurologist to get information about the anti-seizure medication and what signs to look for and how long before he could come off the medication. I requested he be taken off the medication prior to his second birthday. To this day, age 16, he's never had a seizure, to God be the glory!

Facing these obstacles, I never wavered when it came to my child's healing. He was periodically tested up until age six. By the age of three, he had exceeded their expectations and was academically ahead of his age group. After all the years of attending church, being under "the Word," realization hit me, hard. I was angry with myself. All those years in the church, I heard multiple messages on speaking God's Word over your life or situations, and yet, I went through so many years in pain. I heard the Word, but didn't listen and barely read the Bible. My answer was in me all along. I was too distracted with what others spoke over me, and I began to believe them, that something was wrong with me. It took me many years to love myself for who I am. Granted some changes could be made, but they needed to start on the inside. The anger, hurt, distrust and lack of self-worth had turned my insides to ice. I became crude and whatever was on my mind came out my mouth. I thought getting baptized a third time would work and I expected the forgiveness and feelings of trust and comfort to wash over me like a flood, but that didn't happen. I still harbored the same unhealthy feelings toward those closest to me. The feelings of inferiority and spite were still in my heart. Some of the venom I spewed had begun to dissipate and I could feel a change, but it just wasn't happening fast enough for me. The more I prayed, read the Word, daily devotions and affirmations, the better I felt. (Matthew 4:4 KJV) Finally, light filtered through. A graceful breath gushed over me. I finally realized that the trust and faith I had spoken over my son's healing, equipped me to do the same over my life. Releasing the searing pain I'd carried for so many years was like stepping outside into the fresh breeze after a hard rain. I've always felt comfortable praying for others but felt selfish and unworthy to pray for myself. This trick of the "enemy" bound me for many years. Not anymore! One of the most important things I've learned is that I have power in my words.

IN CONCLUSION

We experience many chapters in our individual and collective lives. In fact, you are walking through a chapter in your life right at this very moment. It is our sincere prayer that you know that you are not alone. In the King James Version of the bible, in the book of James 4:8a, we are given the promise to "Draw nigh to God, and He will draw nigh to you."

In each chapter of your life, whether good, bad, and dare we say ugly, it is our prayer that you will choose to allow God to guide you through with grace, peace, joy and love. If you are experiencing a hightide or having a valley low moment, we want you to know that God loves you and that He is right there with you.

In closing, if you are reading this book, then it is not too late for your life to turn around. God never promised us that life would be easy always, but, He did say that He would not leave us alone or comfortless. If you are ready to make a change in your life, we ask that you say this simple prayer with us now.

"Lord, I ask that you come into my heart. I want to live for you. I am ready for my life to be transformed. Dear God, I believe in your son Jesus, that he died on the cross for my sins, and rose on the 3rd day with all power in His hands. And because He has victory, I have victory. I repent of my sins today. Make me new in You. I receive Your love. In Jesus name, Amen."

ACKNOWLEDGEMENT

On behalf of the "I Am Created To Win" authors, we would like to thank our families, friends, Pastor & church family, co-workers and all who played a role in this amazing journey. Your encouragement, patience and support throughout this process have been such a blessing to us. Words simply cannot express our gratitude!

To our editor, Darlene Dunn, thank you for your professional advice and assistance in polishing this book. To our book cover illustrator, Michaela McCormick, thank you for your beautiful gifts and amazing talents, as your picture depicts women everywhere.

Last, but surely not least, we are so grateful to God and humbled that He has chosen us. It is because He has created us to win that we are able to share these very special chapters of our lives. May God be glorified!

Made in the USA
Columbia, SC
23 March 2020